AWESOME DINOSAURS

Illustrated by:
Norma Burgin, Mark Dolby, Graham Kennedy, Peter Komarnysky,
Damian Quayle, Neil Reed, Pete Roberts (Allied Artists), James Field,
Terry Riley (SGA), Mike Atkinson, Chris Forsey, Rob Shone
Cover and title page illustration by Jon Hughes and Russell Gooday
Design by Blue Sunflower Creative

This edition published by Parragon in 2009

Parragon
Queen Street House
4 Queen Street
Bath BA1 1HE, UK

Copyright © Parragon Books Ltd 2008

ISBN 978-1-4075-7503-2

Printed in China

AWESOME DINOSAURS

LIVE. LEARN. DISCOVER.

PaRragon
Bath · New York · Singapore · Hong Kong · Cologne · Delhi · Melbourne

WHAT'S ON THE PAGE

The pages of this book are packed with super stats, fantastic facts and awesome prehistoric monsters. Here's what you'll find on each page!

Defense Factor: This rating tells you how well the dinosaur could defend itself against predators.

Fear Factor: This rating tells you how scary the dinosaur was.

Dinosaur name

Dinosaur nickname

Introduction

Visual key: This shows how big the dinosaur would be compared to an adult human.

Fact File: Find out every crucial stat about the dinosaur here.

ANKYLOSAURUS

Armored Warrior

Ankylosaurus was one of the largest of the armored dinosaurs. If attacked it could deliver a lethal blow with the heavy club at the end of its tail.

Fact File

LENGTH: 33 feet
WEIGHT: 2.2 tons
NAME MEANS: "Stiff lizard"
PRONUNCIATION: Ann-kye-low-sore-uss
DINOSAUR FAMILY: Ankylosaurs
TIME PERIOD: 70 million years ago
FOSSILS FOUND: U.S., Canada
HABITAT: Open woodland
FAVORITE FOOD: Low-growing plants, no more than 6.5 feet off the ground
FEEDING METHOD: It nipped and tugged at pla with its wide beak, then ground its food u many small chewing teeth before swallowing A big tongue helped the dinosaur push the food around its mouth.

10

Visual key: The cool visual key at the top right of each page is a quick reference telling you what type of dinosaur you're looking at. *Ankylosaurus* is an armored plant-eater.

 Killer or scavenger

Giant plant-eater

Armored plant-eater

 Fast bird-footed plant-eater

 Other prehistoric reptile

Special Features: This lists the key features of this dinosaur.

DiscoveryFact™: Check out a weird and wonderful fact about the dino here!

Discovery Rating
Fear Factor: 5/10
Defense Factor: 9/10

Special Features:
- Back side, head, face, and even eyelids covered with thick plates of bony material
- Rows of spines along its back
- Horns at the back of its head
- Heavy club at the end of its tail for use as a weapon

DiscoveryFact™

Ankylosaurus was twice as wide was they were tall.

11

Watch out for surprise pages of jokes, quizzes and dino activities!

ALBERTOSAURUS

Canadian Monster

Albertosaurus was a fierce predator, a fast runner, and a relative of *Tyrannosaurus rex*. The dinosaurs may have hunted in packs, with younger, faster dinosaurs chasing prey into the jaws of slower but larger ones. Put it this way: you wouldn't want to be chased by a pack of these monsters!

Special Features:

- Eyes on the sides of its head
- Probably had a good sense of smell
- Walked on two strong legs
- Two small horns in front of its eyes

Fact File

LENGTH: 29.5 feet

WEIGHT: 2.2 tons

NAME MEANS: "Lizard from Alberta"

PRONUNCIATION: Al-bert-owe-sore-uss

DINOSAUR FAMILY: Tyrannosaurs

TIME PERIOD: 70 million years ago

FOSSILS FOUND: U.S.

HABITAT: Open woodland

FAVORITE FOOD: Fresh or decaying meat, especially *Edmontosaurus*, *Saurolophus*, *Hypacrosaurus* and *Stegoceras* dinosaurs

FEEDING METHOD: Huge banana-shaped teeth that punctured and gripped its unfortunate prey. The dinosaur probably swallowed its food in chunks rather than chewing it.

DiscoveryFact™

Albertosaurus could probably run at speeds of up to 18 miles per hour.

ALLOSAURUS

Massive Meat-Eater

Allosaurus was the largest meat-eater of its time. These terrifying dinosaurs hunted smaller prey on their own, but may have banded together in packs to take down dinosaurs larger than themselves.

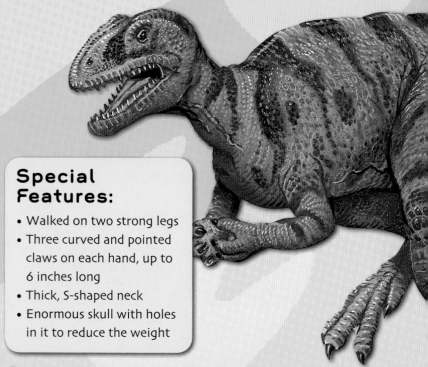

Special Features:

- Walked on two strong legs
- Three curved and pointed claws on each hand, up to 6 inches long
- Thick, S-shaped neck
- Enormous skull with holes in it to reduce the weight

Fact File

LENGTH: 40 feet

WEIGHT: 2.2-5.5 tons

NAME MEANS: "Different lizard"

PRONUNCIATION: Al-owe-sore-uss

DINOSAUR FAMILY: Carnosaurs

TIME PERIOD: 140 million years ago

FOSSILS FOUND: U.S., Portugal, Australia, Africa

HABITAT: Plains and lowlands

FAVORITE FOOD: Medium-sized and large animals. A pack of *Allosaurus* dinosaurs might have been fierce enough to kill huge sauropod dinosaurs such as *Camarasaurus*.

FEEDING METHOD: Imagine a mouth full of 4-inch steak knives. Each tooth was serrated and pointed backwards—they could slice through meat like butter!

DiscoveryFact™

In 1927 the fossils of dozens of *Allosaurus* dinosaurs were discovered very close together in Utah. That's why experts think they may have hunted in packs.

9

ANKYLOSAURUS

Armored Warrior

Ankylosaurus was one of the largest of the armored dinosaurs. If attacked it could deliver a lethal blow with the heavy club at the end of its tail.

Fact File

LENGTH: 33 feet

WEIGHT: 2.2 tons

NAME MEANS: "Stiff lizard"

PRONUNCIATION: Ann-kye-low-sore-uss

DINOSAUR FAMILY: Ankylosaurs

TIME PERIOD: 70 million years ago

FOSSILS FOUND: U.S., Canada

HABITAT: Open woodland

FAVORITE FOOD: Low-growing plants, no more than 6.5 feet off the ground

FEEDING METHOD: It nipped and tugged at plants with its wide beak, then ground its food up with many small chewing teeth before swallowing. A big tongue helped the dinosaur push the food around its mouth.

Special Features:

- Back side, head, face, and even eyelids covered with thick plates of bony material
- Rows of spines along its back
- Horns at the back of its head
- Heavy club at the end of its tail for use as a weapon

DiscoveryFact™

Ankylosaurus was twice as wide was they were tall.

11

APATOSAURUS

Long Lizard

This massive plant-eater had a long neck and a long tail to counterbalance it, like a suspension bridge. If it was attacked it might have used its tail like a whip to lash out and defend itself.

Discovery Rating

Fear Factor: 4/10
Defense Factor: 8/10

Special Features:

- Tail reinforced with extra bones to counterbalance the long neck
- Small head and tiny brain
- Nostrils on top of head
- Front legs shorter than back legs
- Toes of the back feet ended in claws

DiscoveryFact™

Apatosaurus is the scientific name for the dinosaur originally called *Brontosaurus*.

Fact File

LENGTH: 69 feet

WEIGHT: 33 tons

NAME MEANS: "Deceptive lizard"

PRONUNCIATION: Ap-at-oh-sore-uss

DINOSAUR FAMILY: Sauropods

TIME PERIOD: 150 million years ago

FOSSILS FOUND: U.S., Mexico

HABITAT: Lowland floodplains

FAVORITE FOOD: Any part of most types of plant

FEEDING METHOD: Small, pencil-like teeth that nipped away at leaves, twigs, and stems all day, every day. The dinosaur deliberately swallowed stones, which then settled in its stomach and crushed the food it ate into a digestible pulp.

BARYONYX

Expert Fisher

A fossil of this large fish-eating predator was discovered for the first time less than 30 years ago, by an amateur fossil-hunter. The discovery of this new type of dinosaur was a major event.

Fact File

LENGTH: 33 feet

WEIGHT: 2.2 tons

NAME MEANS: "Heavy claw"

PRONUNCIATION: Bare-ee-on-icks

DINOSAUR FAMILY: Baryonychids

TIME PERIOD: 120 million years ago

FOSSILS FOUND: England

HABITAT: Marshy, open woodland with rivers

FAVORITE FOOD: Fish, possibly also dead and decaying animals

FEEDING METHOD: It fished in rivers and lakes. Sharp claws and teeth and a spoon-shaped tip at the end of the skull to scoop up fish helped the dinosaur seize its slippery prey.

DiscoveryFact™

When *Baryonyx* was excavated the remains of its last meal were found in its stomach—a type of fish called *Lepidotes* that grew more than 3 feet long.

Special Features:

- Curved claw on each of its inside fingers that was longer than 1 foot
- Narrow head with a long snout like a crocodile
- Straight neck (most carnivores had S-shaped necks)
- Long, straight tail
- Walked on two legs

BRACHIOSAURUS

Dino-Giraffe

These huge, graceful dinosaurs probably lived in herds and spent most of their time looking for food.

Discovery Rating
Fear Factor: 4/10
Defense Factor: 7/10

Special Features:

- Incredibly long neck
- Short tail
- Small head and tiny brain
- Front legs longer than back legs
- Large nostrils, which means it may have had a good sense of smell

Fact File

LENGTH: 82 feet

WEIGHT: 33-55 tons

NAME MEANS: "Arm lizard"

PRONUNCIATION: Brack-ee-owe-sore-uss

DINOSAUR FAMILY: Sauropods

TIME PERIOD: 150 million years ago

FOSSILS FOUND: Western North America, south-west Europe, north and east Africa

HABITAT: Open woodland

FAVORITE FOOD: Leaves from ginkgo trees, conifer needles, palm fronds, and horsetails

FEEDING METHOD: *Brachiosaurus* may have reared up on its back legs and stretched its neck high into the air to reach leaves at the top of tall trees, or kept all four legs firmly on the ground and swept its neck from side to side to graze low-growing plants. The food was swallowed whole and inside its stomach stones crushed the leaves to a pulp.

DiscoveryFact™

To stay alive, a *Brachiosaurus* would have had to eat more than 440 pounds of plants a day.

ODD ONE OUT

Pick the odd one out!

1. Which of the following was not a carnivore?
(a) Coelophysis
(b) Camarasaurus
(c) Tyrannosaurus rex

2. Which one of these creatures did not live on land?
(a) Elasmosaurus
(b) Euoplocephalus
(c) Brachiosaurus

3. Which one of these creatures could not fly?
(a) *Peteinosaurus*
(b) *Lycorhinus*
(c) *Pterodactylus*

4. Which one of these dinosaurs did not walk on four legs?
(a) *Hypsilophodon*
(b) *Euoplocephalus*
(c) *Brachiosaurus*

5. Which one of these predators did not have any teeth?
(a) *Allosaurus*
(b) *Velociraptor*
(c) *Oviraptor*

Answers on page 96!

CAMARASAURUS

Tough Stuff

While other plant-eaters grazed on the soft, juicy parts of plants, herd-living *Camarasaurus* dinosaurs specialized in eating tough twigs and branches.

Fact File

LENGTH: 60 feet

WEIGHT: 20 tons

NAME MEANS: "Chambered lizard"

PRONUNCIATION: Cam-are-ah-sore-uss

DINOSAUR FAMILY: Sauropods

TIME PERIOD: 150 million years ago

FOSSILS FOUND: U.S., possibly Portugal

HABITAT: Forests

FAVORITE FOOD: Twigs and branches

FEEDING METHOD: Strong jaws and wide, spoon-shaped teeth that pointed forwards allowed Camarasaurus to cut through tough, woody vegetation. Inside its stomach, stones crushed this tough food to a pulp.

DiscoveryFact™

Fossilized bones of *Camarasaurus* have been found with grooves scratched into them, which experts believe were made by the teeth of meat-eaters such as *Allosaurus*.

Discovery Rating
Fear Factor: 3/10
Defense Factor: 5/10

Special Features:

- Small, long head with a blunt, round snout
- Holes in its skull to help reduce the weight
- Spoon-shaped teeth over 1.5 inches wide
- Front and back legs the same size
- Big eyes and big nostrils, which means it probably had good eyesight and a good sense of smell

COELOPHYSIS

Speedy Killer

This small but agile and speedy predator may have been a pack animal, living and hunting in groups.

Fact File

LENGTH: 10 feet

WEIGHT: 88 pounds

NAME MEANS: "Hollow form"

PRONUNCIATION: See-low-fye-siss

DINOSAUR FAMILY: Theropods

TIME PERIOD: 220 million years ago

FOSSILS FOUND: U.S.

HABITAT: Dry, semi-desert habitat

FAVORITE FOOD: Small animals, insects, maybe fish

FEEDING METHOD: *Coelophysis* chased after prey and probably used its front legs to claw and grasp at food. It might also have dug in the ground for grubs and worms.

DiscoveryFact™

Coelophysis was one of the first-ever meat-eating dinosaurs. It lived 150 million years before *Tyrannosaurus rex*.

Special Features:

- Ran on two powerful back legs
- Hollow leg bones, which kept its weight down and allowed it to move quickly
- Long, flexible neck
- Long, beak-like jaws full of sharp teeth

23

CORYTHOSAURUS

Helmet Head

The *Corythosaurus* dinosaur's amazing "helmet" head crest was hollow, and could have been used to make calls to other dinosaurs, or to improve its sense of smell. Only adult male dinosaurs grew fully developed head crests.

Fact File

LENGTH: 33 feet

WEIGHT: 4.4 tons

NAME MEANS: "Helmet lizard"

PRONUNCIATION: Kor-rih-those-sore-uss

DINOSAUR FAMILY: Hadrosaurs

TIME PERIOD: 80 million years ago

FOSSILS FOUND: U.S., Canada

HABITAT: Swampy lowlands

FAVORITE FOOD: Plants

FEEDING METHOD: The horn-covered bony beak at the front of the mouth was used to grab vegetation, and inside the mouth hundreds of small teeth ground food to a pulp before it was swallowed.

Discovery Rating
Fear Factor: 2/10
Defense Factor: 5/10

Special Features:

- Large, hollow bony crest on top of the head
- Wide, paddle-like hands and feet that may have been webbed
- Horn-covered bony beak
- Hundreds of small teeth (called "dental batteries")

DiscoveryFact™

Corythosaurus dinosaurs may have been able to swim.

DIPLODOCUS

Large but Light

Unlike other sauropods, herd-living *Diplodocus* could not raise its long neck much above shoulder height. If it was attacked it could have used its tail like a whip to lash out and defend itself.

Special Features:

- Long neck, about 26 feet long
- Even longer tail, up to 46 feet long
- Spine bones had hollow spaces, which made the dinosaur surprisingly light for its size
- Back legs longer than front legs

Fact File

LENGTH: 88.5 feet

WEIGHT: 13.3 tons

NAME MEANS: "Double-beam lizard"

PRONUNCIATION: Dip-lod-ock-uss

DINOSAUR FAMILY: Sauropods

TIME PERIOD: 150 million years ago

FOSSILS FOUND: U.S.

HABITAT: Open woodland

FAVORITE FOOD: The leaves of low-growing plants such as ferns and horsetails

FEEDING METHOD: *Diplodocus* had weak, peg-like teeth at the front of its jaws. With a swoop of its head, these forward-facing teeth combed their way through foliage, stripping off mouthfuls of food. Inside its stomach stones crushed the leaves to a pulp.

DiscoveryFact™

The group of dinosaurs called diplodocids were the longest animals ever to walk the Earth.

ELASMOSAURUS

Long-Necked and Lethal

Elasmosaurus probably had to swim quite slowly because of the length of its neck, but it could whip its head around to snatch at prey with lethal speed.

Special Features:

- Neck was over half of its total length
- 70 bones in its neck—many more than most reptiles have. This made the neck very strong and flexible.
- Extra set of ribs in the belly, to anchor the huge muscles needed to work its flippers

Discovery Rating

Fear Factor: 6/10
Defense Factor: 6/10

Fact File

LENGTH: 46 feet

WEIGHT: 2.2 tons

NAME MEANS: "Thin-plated lizard"

PRONUNCIATION: Ee-laz-moe-sore-uss

DINOSAUR FAMILY: Plesiosaurs

TIME PERIOD: 70 million years ago

FOSSILS FOUND: North America

HABITAT: The sea

FAVORITE FOOD: Small creatures like fish, squid and curly-shelled ammonites

FEEDING METHOD: *Elasmosaurus* whipped its head around to snap up whole schools of its prey in one gulp. Long teeth trapped the food in its mouth.

DiscoveryFact™

Some people say that plesiosaurs could still survive today in deep, remote lakes, and that the mythical Loch Ness Monster in Scotland could be one.

EUDIMORPHODON

Fine Flier

This small, powerful flier might have used its strong claws to cling to a cliff face or tree between flights, as bats do today. Young *Eudimorphodon* pterosaurs may have snapped up flying insects, while the adults probably ate fish.

DiscoveryFact™

Eudimorphodon—"true two-form tooth"—got its name because it had two kinds of teeth—sharp fangs at the front and smaller teeth with three or five points at the back. No other pterosaur had teeth like this.

Special Features:

- Strong wing-flapping muscles
- Three short, strong fingers and claws on each wing
- Three pairs of large openings in the skull, to reduce weight
- Long jaws and sharp teeth
- Long tail with a paddle at the end

Fact File

LENGTH: 3.3 feet

WEIGHT: 0.5 pounds

NAME MEANS: "True two-form tooth"

PRONUNCIATION: You-di-morf-o-don

DINOSAUR FAMILY: Pterosaurs

TIME PERIOD: 220 million years ago

FOSSILS FOUND: Italy

HABITAT: Around rivers and lakes

FAVORITE FOOD: Fish, insects

FEEDING METHOD: *Eudimorphodon* flew low over the water, swooping and turning to peer for shadowy fish under the surface. It may have caught its fishy food by plunging like an arrow into the water, as some birds do today. Sharp teeth helped to catch its slippery prey.

31

ANCIENT ANAGRAMS

Each of these phrases is the mixed-up name of a dinosaur! Can you work out which is which?

1. Sauce Pope Hullo

2. Annoy Surtax Surer

3. Hidden Moo Pour

4. Lucid Do Sop

5. Chair Shuts You

Answers on page 96!

7. Reactors Pit

6. Crystal Pouted

8. A Dog Union

9. Solar Usual

10. Roar Pivot

EUOPLOCEPHALUS

Forest Fighter

Euoplocephalus dinosaurs may have lived in herds. Like *Ankylosaurus*, they spent most of their time feeding peacefully, but could defend themselves very effectively if attacked.

Fact File

LENGTH: 23 feet

WEIGHT: 2.2 tons

NAME MEANS: "Well-armored head"

PRONUNCIATION: You-oh-ploe-seff-ah-luss

DINOSAUR FAMILY: Ankylosaurs

TIME PERIOD: 70 million years ago

FOSSILS FOUND: U.S., Canada

HABITAT: Forests

FAVORITE FOOD: Low-growing plants

FEEDING METHOD: Its wide beak was used to grab vegetation. Many tiny teeth crushed the twigs and leaves before swallowing.

Discovery Rating
Fear Factor: 4/10
Defense Factor: 8 /10

Special Features:

- Bands of armour plating across its back, embedded into its leathery skin
- Armored head plated and covered with bony knobs
- Rows of spines along its back
- Four horns to guard its neck
- Heavy tail club to use as a weapon

DiscoveryFact™

The ankylosaurs' name means "fused lizards." They are called this because plates of bony armour were fused together over their bodies.

HYPSILOPHODON

Swift Sprinter

The main defense *Hypsilophodon* dinosaurs had against predators was to run away—really fast! They may have been able to reach 25 miles per hour over short distances. Like antelopes or gazelles today, the dinosaurs also lived in herds to protect themselves.

Special Features:

- Stiff tail held out straight behind it
- Moved on two long slender hind legs
- Bony beak, ridged, chisel-like teeth and cheek pouches
- Large eyes

DiscoveryFact™

Camels and cows today grind their food down in the same way that *Hypsilophodon* dinosaurs did.

Fact File

LENGTH: 7.5 feet

WEIGHT: 155 pounds

NAME MEANS: "High ridge tooth"

PRONUNCIATION: Hip-sill-owe-foe-don

DINOSAUR FAMILY: Hypsilophodonts

TIME PERIOD: 120 million years ago

FOSSILS FOUND: England, Spain, possibly U.S.

HABITAT: Floodplains

FAVORITE FOOD: Low-growing plants such as ferns and horsetails. The dinosaurs probably only ate the tender shoots and leaves.

FEEDING METHOD: A bony beak at the front of the mouth was used to slice through vegetation. Plant material was then pushed into the dinosaur's cheek pouches using the long tongue, and ridged chewing teeth began to grind away at the food, quickly reducing it to a juicy pulp that was easy to swallow.

ICHTHYOSAURUS

Streamlined Swimmer

This speedy, streamlined sea-dweller looked similar to a modern dolphin and probably lived a similar lifestyle.

DiscoveryFact™

Hundreds of fossils of *Ichthyosaurus* have been found, some with every bone perfectly preserved and even traces of flesh.

Special Features:

- Back fin and a tail
- Big eyes, to help it spot prey in the gloom of the deep ocean
- Long, narrow jaws with many sharp teeth

Fact File

LENGTH: 6 feet

WEIGHT: 200 pounds

NAME MEANS: "Fish lizard"

PRONUNCIATION: Ick-thee-owe-sore-uss

DINOSAUR FAMILY: Ichthyosaurs

TIME PERIOD: 200 million years ago

FOSSILS FOUND: Mainly Europe

HABITAT: The sea

FAVORITE FOOD: Mainly fish, but also squid, long-bodied belemites and curly-shelled ammonites

FEEDING METHOD: *Ichthyosaurus* was a slim, sleek, speedy swimmer that chased and snapped up prey using its sharp teeth and narrow jaws. It may have been able to hold its breath and dive to great depths in search of prey.

IGUANODON

Special Features:

- Four clawed fingers and a big spiked thumb
- Blunt, toothless beak covered with a layer of horn
- Many tightly packed chewing teeth
- Three-toed feet with hooves

DiscoveryFact™

Iguanodon was the second dinosaur ever named, when Victorian fossil collector Dr. Gideon Mantell (1790-1852) realized that the fossilized tooth he had was similar to that of a modern-day iguana.

Iguanodon could walk on either two or four legs. It probably lived in herds, and used its big spiked thumb for self-defense against predators, or in disputes within the herd.

Fact File

LENGTH: 33 feet

WEIGHT: 5.5 tons

NAME MEANS: "Iguana tooth"

PRONUNCIATION: Ig-wan-oh-don

DINOSAUR FAMILY: Iguanodonts

TIME PERIOD: 130 million years ago

FOSSILS FOUND: Europe, possibly North America

HABITAT: Woodland

FAVORITE FOOD: Leaves, stems, fruit, and seeds

FEEDING METHOD: It used its tough beak to grab vegetation, then long, sharp chewing teeth ground the plants down to a mushy pulp. Its tongue continually moved food around inside its mouth, into and out of its cheek pouches, until it was ready to be swallowed.

Discovery Rating
Fear Factor: 2/10
Defense Factor: 5/10

KENTROSAURUS

Plated Dinosaur

This slow-moving dinosaur protected itself with sharp spines growing from its tail and hips. The plates on the front half of its body were probably used for courtship displays or to help control body temperature.

DiscoveryFact™

Kentrosaurus's brain was no bigger than a walnut!

Special Features:

- Two rows of bony plates embedded into the skin of its back
- Seven pairs of spines running from its mid-section to the tip of its tail
- Spine protecting each hip
- Small, narrow head and tiny brain

Fact File

LENGTH: 16 feet

WEIGHT: 1.1 tons

NAME MEANS: "Spiked lizard"

PRONUNCIATION: Ken-troe-sore-uss

DINOSAUR FAMILY: Stegosaurs

TIME PERIOD: 155 million years ago

FOSSILS FOUND: Tanzania

HABITAT: Coastal plains

FAVORITE FOOD: Low-growing plants

FEEDING METHOD: It used its toothless beak to gather vegetation. Then small, weak teeth chewed and crushed the plants before swallowing. The dinosaur may also have reared up on its back legs to reach food.

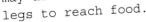

LIOPLEURODON

Colossal Predator

This terrifying sea-monster tracked prey like sharks do today. If the scent of prey was stronger in one nostril than the other, *Liopleurodon* would veer to that side and follow the trail.

Fact File

LENGTH: 82 feet

WEIGHT: 83-165 tons

NAME MEANS: "Smooth-sided tooth"

PRONUNCIATION: Lie-owe-plure-owe-don

DINOSAUR FAMILY: Pliosaurs

TIME PERIOD: 150 million years ago

FOSSILS FOUND: Europe, possibly South America

HABITAT: The sea

FAVORITE FOOD: Fish or squid for a light snack, other sea-living reptiles like ichthyosaurs, plesiosaurs and pliosaurs for a main meal

FEEDING METHOD: Despite its size, *Liopleurodon* could move swiftly through the water when chasing prey. It seized food using two huge rows of curved, deadly teeth.

Discovery Rating

Fear Factor: 10/10
Defense Factor: 9/10

Special Features:

- A skull more than 16 feet long
- Two rows of curved teeth, each 1 foot long
- Rear flippers larger than front flippers
- Openings between roof of mouth and nostrils, to help track prey

DiscoveryFact™

Liopleurodon was the largest meat-eater ever to live on our planet.

LYCORHINUS

Tusk-like Teeth

Discovery Rating
Fear Factor: 1/10
Defense Factor: 1/10

DiscoveryFact™

Only *Lycorhinus*'s teeth have ever been found. That's why we're not sure how long it was or how much it weighed

Special Features:
- Large, slightly curved tusk-like teeth in its upper and lower jaws
- Bony beak, cheek pouches, and many small teeth
- Large hands and clawed fingers

This small dinosaur is known for having unusual tusk-like teeth. Experts think they were probably not used for biting into meat, but for courtship or in fights with other *Lycorhinus* dinosaurs.

Fact File

LENGTH: 4 feet (uncertain)

WEIGHT: unknown

NAME MEANS: "Wolf snout"

PRONUNCIATION: Liek-oh-rien-us

DINOSAUR FAMILY: Heterodontosaurs

TIME PERIOD: 200 million years ago

FOSSILS FOUND: South Africa

FAVORITE FOOD: Low-growing plants, edible roots and tubers, possibly also small insects and burrow-living animals

FEEDING METHOD: It ate low-growing plants, but also probably dug for edible roots, tubers, and possibly even small insects and other creatures using its large hands and clawed fingers.

47

WHO AM I?

Can you guess who's talking?

1. I was the largest meat-eater of my time, and my name means "different lizard."

2. I was a fish-eater with a 1-foot curved claw on my thumbs, and my bones were found in England.

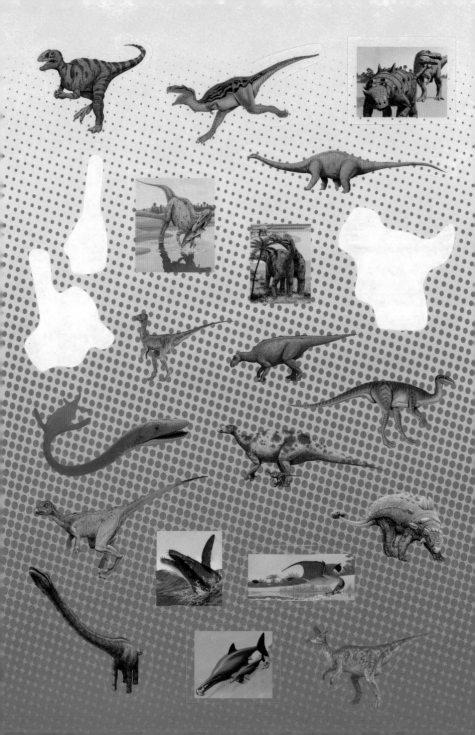

3. I was small but nasty, and I hunted in packs. I was a clever animal, and I had serrated teeth and a large, sickle-shaped claw on each foot.

4. I lived in the sea, and had a fin and tail like a dolphin. My name means "fish lizard."

Answers on page 96!

5. I lived in the desert. I ate small prey and had a short beak and a layer of fluffy down on my body. I took good care of my eggs and young.

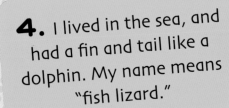

MAIASAURA

Mother Lizard

Maiasaura dinosaurs lived in enormous herds of as many as 10,000 animals. They nested together in vast colonies, and took good care of their eggs and young.

Discovery Rating
Fear Factor: 3/10
Defense Factor: 6/10

Fact File

LENGTH: 29.5 feet

WEIGHT: 3.3 tons

NAME MEANS: "Good mother lizard"

PRONUNCIATION: My-yah-sore-ah

DINOSAUR FAMILY: Hadrosaurs

TIME PERIOD: 80 million years ago

FOSSILS FOUND: North America

HABITAT: Open plains rich in vegetation

FAVORITE FOOD: Plants

FEEDING METHOD: *Maiasaura* dinosaurs gathered plants with their wide beaks and crushed food with the many small teeth inside their mouths before swallowing. As the herds were so large, they would have had to stay constantly on the move to find enough food.

Special Features:
- Bony crest on top of the head
- Long head, a similar shape to a horse's today

DiscoveryFact™

The place in Montana where thousands of fossils of *Maiasaura* eggs, nests and babies were found has been nicknamed "Egg Mountain."

OVIRAPTOR

Fluffy but Nasty

Many *Oviraptor* fossils have been discovered with eggs, both its own and those of other dinosaurs. Like *Maiasaura* it probably took good care of its eggs and young—but it may also have sneakily raided the nests of other dinosaurs!

Fact File

LENGTH: 6 feet

WEIGHT: 44 pounds

NAME MEANS: "Egg thief"

PRONUNCIATION: Owe-vee-rap-tore

DINOSAUR FAMILY: Oviraptors

TIME PERIOD: 80 million years ago

FOSSILS FOUND: Mongolia, possibly China

HABITAT: Dry, semi-desert environment

FAVORITE FOOD: Uncertain. Possibly eggs, or possibly small prey. It may even have eaten plants.

FEEDING METHOD: *Oviraptor* might have raided the nests of other dinosaurs and crushed the eggs with its strong beak. Or it could have chased small prey and killed it with pecks from its beak and kicks.

Special Features:

- Tall, bony crest
- A short beak without any teeth
- Three fingers on each hand, ending in strong, curved claws each about 3 inches long

DiscoveryFact™

Oviraptor was probably covered in a layer of fluffy down and may even have had feathers.

53

PACHYCEPHALOSAURUS

Hard-Headed

Discovery Rating
Fear Factor: 4/10
Defense Factor: 6/10

The amazingly tough heads of these dinosaurs might have been used for defense, or in battles over mates or to decide which dinosaur would lead the herd.

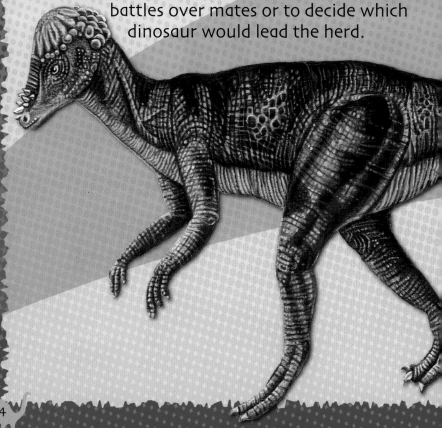

Fact File

LENGTH: 15 feet (uncertain)

WEIGHT: 660 pounds (uncertain)

NAME MEANS: "Thick-headed lizard"

PRONUNCIATION: Pak-ee-seff-ah-low-sore-uss

DINOSAUR FAMILY: Pachycephalosaurs

TIME PERIOD: 70 million years ago

FOSSILS FOUND: U.S., possibly Canada

HABITAT: Forests

FAVORITE FOOD: Probably leaves and fruit

FEEDING METHOD: It munched on the soft parts of plants with its small, pointed, and fairly weak teeth.

Special Features:

- Huge skull, 2 feet long and with a dome on top that could be 10 inches of solid bone
- Bony nodules projecting from its snout and from the back of its head
- Many tiny teeth packed into its jaws

DiscoveryFact™

Only the skull of *Pachycephalosaurus* has ever been found. That's why we're not sure how long it was or how much it weighed.

55

PARASAUROLOPHUS

Head-Crested

Experts think that *Parasaurolophus* may have used its hollow head crest, which was connected to its nose and throat, to make a a deep trumpeting noise.

DiscoveryFact™

Parasaurolophus's crest was about 3 feet long.

Special Features:

- Long, hollow head crest
- Notch in the backbone that was a resting place for the crest when the dinosaur tipped its head back
- Thick, wrinkled skin covered by a "pavement" of small, overlapping bony plates

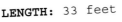

Fact File

LENGTH: 33 feet

WEIGHT: 4 tons

NAME MEANS: "Beside Saurolophus"

PRONUNCIATION: Para-sore-owe-loaf-uss

DINOSAUR FAMILY: Hadrosaurs

TIME PERIOD: 70 million years ago

FOSSILS FOUND: U.S., Canada

HABITAT: Woodland and river banks

FAVORITE FOOD: Plants

FEEDING METHOD: Hundreds of teeth pulverized plant food before the dinosaur swallowed it.

PETEINOSAURUS

Flying Jaws

This small pterosaur was about the size of a pigeon—but much fiercer! Its head was only the size of a thumb, but it was mostly jaws, full of sharp teeth.

Discovery Rating
Fear Factor: 2/10
Defense Factor: 3/10

Special Features:

- Two large front fangs
- A long tail with a "paddle" at the end, which it used as a rudder to steer in flight
- Tail bones stiffened by bony rods

Fact File

WINGSPAN: 2 feet

WEIGHT: 0.25 pounds

NAME MEANS: "Winged lizard"

PRONUNCIATION: Pet-ine-oh-saw-rus

DINOSAUR FAMILY: Pterosaurs

TIME PERIOD: 220 million years ago

FOSSILS FOUND: Italy

HABITAT: Seashores

FAVORITE FOOD: Insects such as dragonflies

FEEDING METHOD: It probably swooped down from a perch and used its two front fangs to grab insects in mid air.

DiscoveryFact™

Peteinosaurus was one of the first creatures to be able to fly by flapping its wings, rather than just gliding.

PLATECARPUS

Mean Mosasaur

Mean mosasaurs, such as *Platecarpus*, were the top predators in the seas for 20 million years. Big, fast and equipped with terrifying teeth, they were much fiercer than sharks are today.

Fact File

LENGTH: 14 feet

WEIGHT: About 880 pounds

NAME MEANS: "Flat-wristed"

PRONUNCIATION: Plat-ee-carp-uss

DINOSAUR FAMILY: Mosasaurs

TIME PERIOD: 70 million years ago

FOSSILS FOUND: Europe, North America

HABITAT: Sea

FAVORITE FOOD: Fish and ammonites

FEEDING METHOD: It moved fast to chase prey through the water by swishing its body from side, like a snake. Its teeth and jaws were strong enough to crack open tough ammonite shells.

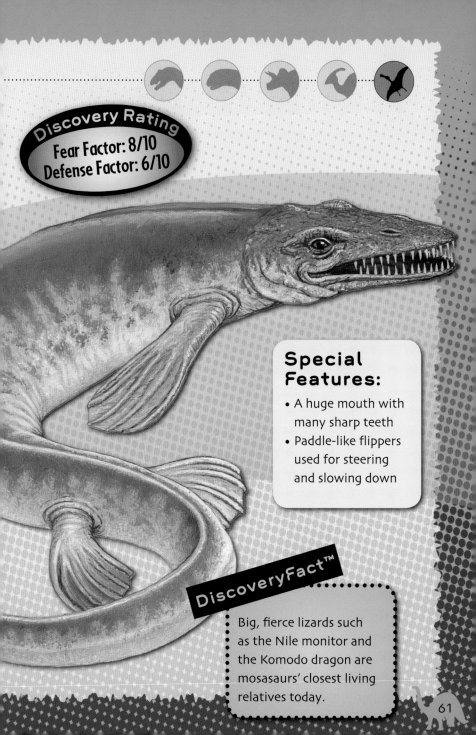

Special Features:

- A huge mouth with many sharp teeth
- Paddle-like flippers used for steering and slowing down

DiscoveryFact™

Big, fierce lizards such as the Nile monitor and the Komodo dragon are mosasaurs' closest living relatives today.

61

PLATEOSAURUS

Rearing Up

Plateosaurus was one of the largest land animals of its time. These dinosaurs probably moved around in herds for protection.

Fact File

LENGTH: 23 feet

WEIGHT: 2.2 tons

NAME MEANS: "Flat reptile"

PRONUNCIATION: Plat-ee-owe-sore-uss

DINOSAUR FAMILY: Prosauropods

TIME PERIOD: 220 million years ago

FOSSILS FOUND: France, Germany, Switzerland

HABITAT: Dry, semi-desert

FAVORITE FOOD: Softer leaves and fronds

FEEDING METHOD: It reared up on its back legs to reach the tree tops and find food. Inside its mouth were around 120 small, leaf-shaped teeth for slicing off leaves, which it probably swallowed whole.

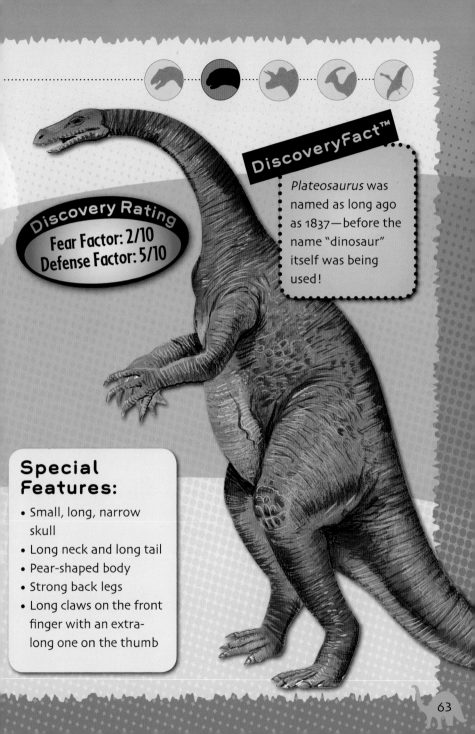

Plateosaurus was named as long ago as 1837—before the name "dinosaur" itself was being used!

Discovery Rating
Fear Factor: 2/10
Defense Factor: 5/10

Special Features:

- Small, long, narrow skull
- Long neck and long tail
- Pear-shaped body
- Strong back legs
- Long claws on the front finger with an extra-long one on the thumb

DINO JOKES!

What do you get when you cross a dinosaur and a mole?

A very big hole in your garden

What do you get when dinosaurs crash cars?

Tyrannosaurus Wrecks!

What do you call a fossil that doesn't want to work?

Lazy Bones!

What do you call a sleeping dinosaur?

A Bronto-snore-us!

What do you call a dinosaur that is fast asleep?

A Stego-snor-us

What do you call a dinosaur who's been on a 15-mile walk?

A Myfeetaresoreus

What would a T-rex say to you?

Pleased to meat you!

What sort of T-shirts do dinosaurs wear?

Tricera-tops!

PROTOCERATOPS

Nesting Dino

This small ceratopsid had a bony neck frill to protect the soft skin around the neck. We know that the dinosaurs built nests, and probably took good care of their eggs and young.

Discovery Rating
Fear Factor: 3/10
Defense Factor: 5/10

Fact File

LENGTH: 6 feet

WEIGHT: 400 pounds

NAME MEANS: "First horned face"

PRONUNCIATION: Proe-toe-serra-tops

DINOSAUR FAMILY: Ceratopsids

TIME PERIOD: 70 million years ago

FOSSILS FOUND: Mongolia

HABITAT: Dry, semi-desert

FAVORITE FOOD: Plants

FEEDING METHOD: *Protoceratops* bit through plant material with its beak, then chewed it into smaller pieces before swallowing it.

Special Features:

- Bony neck frill
- Bump on its snout
- A beak-like snout, like that of a parrot (as ceratopsids all had)

DiscoveryFact™

One amazing fossil find shows a *Protoceratops* actually in the act of battling a *Velociraptor* dinosaur!

PSITTACOSAURUS

Parrot Lizard

This dinosaur probably walked on two legs and was a fast runner. *Psittacosaurus* lived on the Earth for over 30 million years, which makes it one of the longest-lived dino species.

Special Features:

- Prominent cheek bones
- Particularly powerful beak-like snout (all ceratopsids had these)
- Lightly built
- Only four fingers on each hand (other ceratopsids had five)

Discovery Rating
Fear Factor: 3/10
Defense Factor: 3/10

Fact File

LENGTH: 8 feet

WEIGHT: 110 pounds

NAME MEANS: "Parrot lizard"

PRONUNCIATION: Sit-ah-coe-sore-uss

DINOSAUR FAMILY: Ceratopsids

TIME PERIOD: 130 million years ago

FOSSILS FOUND: Mongolia, China, Thailand

HABITAT: Dry, semi-desert

FAVORITE FOOD: Plants, possibly small prey

FEEDING METHOD: It used its parrot-like beak and sharp teeth to slice through vegetation, but it didn't have any chewing teeth. Stones in the stomach crushed the plants.

DiscoveryFact™

Even back in the Cretaceous period, reptiles weren't always on top. The remains of a young *Psittacosaurus* have been discovered in the stomach of *Repenomamus*, a predatory mammal of the time.

PTERODACTYLUS

Flying Wonder

Many different kinds of *Pterodactylus* have been found, ranging from creatures as small as a blackbird to giants with wing spans of more than 8 feet!

Special Features:

- Short tail
- Long, narrow wings
- Very thin, light bones in its skull
- May have had a furry body

Discovery Rating

Fear Factor: 2/10
Defense Factor: 3/10

Fact File

NAME MEANS: "Winged finger"

PRONUNCIATION: Ter-o-dack-ti-lus

WINGSPAN: 1-8 feet

WEIGHT: Varied

DINOSAUR FAMILY: Pterosaurs

TIME PERIOD: 145 million years ago

FOSSILS FOUND: Germany, France, England, Tanzania

HABITAT: Rivers, lakes

FAVORITE FOOD: Fish, insects

FEEDING METHOD: *Pterodactylus* could catch insects during flight, or swoop down and scoop up fish from a lake or river.

DiscoveryFact™

Pterosaur fingers and toes were ideal for gripping onto branches or ledges. They might have roosted as bats do today—hanging upside down!

71

QUETZALCOATLUS

Plane-sized Pterosaur

Seeing this vast beast swooping towards you out of the skies must have been a terrifying sight!

Fact File

WINGSPAN: 36 feet

WEIGHT: 154-220 pounds

NAME MEANS: "Feathered serpent"

PRONUNCIATION: Kett-zal-coe-at-luss

DINOSAUR FAMILY: Pterosaurs

TIME PERIOD: 70 million years ago

FOSSILS FOUND: U.S., Mexico

HABITAT: Inland, perhaps along rivers and lakes

FAVORITE FOOD: Uncertain. Possibly dead animals, or possibly fish, shellfish and crabs

FEEDING METHOD: If *Quetzalcoatlus* was a scavenger it probably soared high in the air, as vultures and condors do today, watching out for dead and dying animals on the ground. Or it could have crushed shellfish with the edges of its powerful beak.

Special Features:

- Huge—as big as a small plane!
- Sharp, powerful beak
- Big eyes
- Large brain
- May have been covered in fuzzy fur

DiscoveryFact™

Quetzalcoatlus was named after Quetzalcoatl, a god of the ancient Aztec people of Mexico.

73

SEISMOSAURUS

The Ground's Shaking!

It really would have been like being in an earthquake if one of these giants was walking towards you, shaking the ground at every step of its enomous feet. That's why *Seismosaurus* means "Earth-shaking lizard!"

Special Features:

- Long, whip-like tail
- Long neck
- Peg-like teeth
- Nostrils on the top of its head

DiscoveryFact™

Seismosaurus is the longest dinosaur ever discovered.

Fact File

LENGTH: 131 feet

WEIGHT: 33 tons

NAME MEANS: "Earth-shaking lizard"

PRONUNCIATION: Size-mow-sore-uss

DINOSAUR FAMILY: Sauropods

TIME PERIOD: 150 million years ago

FOSSILS FOUND: U.S.

HABITAT: Forests

FAVORITE FOOD: Plants

FEEDING METHOD: It nipped off plant material with its mouth and swallowed it whole. Stones in its stomach ground the food to a digestible pulp.

Discovery Rating

Fear Factor: 3/10

Defense Factor: 8/10

STEGOCERAS

Head-Butt!

Stegoceras dinosaurs lived in herds. They probably head-butted each other in fights over mates, or who would lead the herd.

Fact File

LENGTH: 6.5 feet

WEIGHT: 121 pounds

NAME MEANS: "Horny roof"

PRONUNCIATION: Steg-owe-sair-ass

DINOSAUR FAMILY: Pachycephalosaurs

TIME PERIOD: 70 million years ago

FOSSILS FOUND: U.S., Canada

HABITAT: Open woodland

FAVORITE FOOD: Plants, roots and possibly small insects and mammals

FEEDING METHOD: *Stegoceras* probably grasped at plants with its hands and fingers, and used its finger claws to scratch up roots and other foods such as insects.

DiscoveryFact™

Stegoceras and other pachycephalosaurs had an unusual, hollow piece of bone at the ends of their tails. Experts still don't really know why!

Special Features:

- A long, dome-shaped skull, thick and knobby at the front and over 2 inches thick
- Large eyes
- Many small, sharp teeth
- Long, stiff tail

STEGOSAURUS

Plated Wonder

This slow-moving plant-eater probably lived in small family groups. Experts think that the amazing plates on its back were probably used to help control body temperature.

Fact File

LENGTH: 29.5 feet

WEIGHT: 2.2 tons

NAME MEANS: "Roofed lizard"

PRONUNCIATION: Steg-owe-sore-uss

DINOSAUR FAMILY: Stegosaurs

TIME PERIOD: 150 million years ago

FOSSILS FOUND: U.S.

HABITAT: Open woodland, floodplains

FAVORITE FOOD: Low-growing plants

FEEDING METHOD: *Stegosaurus* always walked on all fours, and gathered low-growing plants with a beak-like horny sheath. Inside its jaws were many small teeth to chew and crush its food before swallowing.

Special Features:

- 17 bony plates along its back, which may have been flat, arranged in pairs or on alternating sides
- Horned tail for defense against predators

Discovery Rating

Fear Factor: 3/10
Defense Factor: 7/10

DiscoveryFact™

Stegosaurus got its name—"roofed lizard"—because at first experts thought that the plates covered its back like the shell of a turtle.

TRUE OR FALSE?

Test your dino knowledge with this quick quiz! Which of the following statements are true and which are false?

1. The pliosaur *Liopleurodon* was probably the largest meat-eating creature ever to live on the Earth.

2. The dinosaur *Baryonyx* ate mainly meat.

4. *Maiasaura* dinosaurs were good mothers.

3. Live dinosaurs can still be found today in parts of China.

5. An *Ankylosaurus* would have been easy prey for a *Tyrannosaurus rex*.

6. *Oviraptor* dinosaurs had deadly teeth.

7. *Tyrannosaurus rex* may have been a scavenger as well as a hunter.

8. All dinosaurs were large animals.

9. *Kentrosaurus* dinosaurs were very clever.

10. *Allosaurus* dinosaurs usually moved on all fours.

Answers on page 96!

STYRACOSAURUS

Frills and Horns

Styracosaurus lived in herds. Its amazing neck frill was partly to protect it from predators, but the dinosaurs also locked heads together and pushed to decide who was the strongest when fighting over mates.

Fact File

LENGTH: 17 feet

WEIGHT: 3 tons

NAME MEANS: "Spiked lizard"

PRONUNCIATION: Sty-rack-owe-sore-uss

DINOSAUR FAMILY: Ceratopsids

TIME PERIOD: 70 million years ago

FOSSILS FOUND: U.S., Canada

HABITAT: Plains and open woodland

FAVORITE FOOD: Low-growing plants

FEEDING METHOD: The dinosaur gathered plants with its beak, and chewed its food well with its many teeth, before swallowing.

Fear Factor: 4/10
Defense Factor: 8/10

DiscoveryFact™

Styracosaurus was surprisingly fast— it could probably run at up to 20 miles per hour.

Special Features:

- Large neck frill with six long horns and several shorter ones
- Straight 2-foot horn on its nose

SUPERSAURUS

Super Lizard

This huge dinosaur may have lived in herds that moved between feeding grounds. The dinosaurs had enormous appetites, and would have spent most of their time eating.

DiscoveryFact™

The shoulder blade alone of a *Supersaurus* is taller than a person—8 feet!

Special Features:

- Long tail counterbalancing a long neck
- Heel cushions on the bottom of its feet, which acted as shock absorbers
- Peg-shaped teeth

Fact File

LENGTH: 138 feet (estimated)
WEIGHT: 60 tons (estimated)
NAME MEANS: "Super lizard"
PRONUNCIATION: Soo-pur-sore-uss
DINOSAUR FAMILY: Sauropods
TIME PERIOD: 150 million years ago
FOSSILS FOUND: U.S.
HABITAT: Open woodland

Discovery Rating
Fear Factor: 3/10
Defense Factor: 9/10

FAVORITE FOOD: Plants

FEEDING METHOD: *Supersaurus* swung its long neck from side to side to gather vast amounts of plant material, which it swallowed whole. Stones in the stomach ground the leaves and twigs to a digestible pulp.

TITANOSAURUS

Titanic Lizard

Titanosaurus's size was its best defense—the force carried by a flick of an adult's tail, or the kick of a leg, would be enough to send even large predators reeling. But the young, the old and the sick were in danger.

Fact File

LENGTH: 66 feet

WEIGHT: 20 tons

NAME MEANS: "Titanic lizard"

PRONUNCIATION: Tie-tan-owe-sore-uss

DINOSAUR FAMILY: Sauropods

TIME PERIOD: 70 million years ago

FOSSILS FOUND: Asia, Africa, Europe, South America

HABITAT: Open woodland

FAVORITE FOOD: Plants

FEEDING METHOD: *Titanosaurus* swallowed its food whole. Stones in the stomach ground the plant material to a digestible pulp.

Special Features:

- Unlike other sauropods, the skin on *Titanosaurus*'s back was studded with small armoured plates
- Long neck
- Whip-like tail

Discovery Rating
Fear Factor: 3/10
Defense Factor: 8/10

DiscoveryFact™

Titanosaurus is named after the mighty Titans of Greek mythology—beings with great strength and power.

TRICERATOPS

Three Horns

Bulky *Triceratops* probably lived in vast herds, hundreds or even thousands strong. Stronger animals protected the weak, the young and the old.

Fact File

LENGTH: 29.5 feet

WEIGHT: 5.5 tons

NAME MEANS: "Three-horned face"

PRONUNCIATION: Try-serra-tops

DINOSAUR FAMILY: Ceratopsids

TIME PERIOD: 70 million years ago

FOSSILS FOUND: U.S.

HABITAT: Open woodland

FAVORITE FOOD: Low-growing plants

FEEDING METHOD: *Triceratops* bit through vegetation with its powerful beak. Chewing teeth cut the food into smaller pieces before being swallowed.

Special Features:

- Large, wavy-edged neck frill made of solid bone
- Three horns
- Powerful hooked beak

Discovery Rating
Fear Factor: 4/10
Defense Factor: 7/10

DiscoveryFact™

Triceratops horns have been found with deep grooves in them that fit the teeth of *Tyrannosaurus rex*!

TYRANNOSAURUS RE✖

Tyrant Lizard

Tyrannosaurus rex was one of the biggest-ever predators on land. Huge and fierce, with teeth up to 8 inches long, a *Tyrannosaurus* would have snapped up a person like a bag of chips!

Discovery Rating
Fear Factor: 10/10
Defense Factor: 8/10

DiscoveryFact™

Tyrannosaurus's mouth was big enough to swallow a person whole!

Fact File

LENGTH: 40 feet

WEIGHT: 8.8 tons

NAME MEANS: "Tyrant lizard"

PRONUNCIATION: Tie-ran-owe-sore-uss

DINOSAUR FAMILY: Tyrannosaurs

TIME PERIOD: 70 million years ago

FOSSILS FOUND: U.S.

HABITAT: Open woodland

FAVORITE FOOD: Meat, either fresh or decaying

FEEDING METHOD: *Tyrannosaurus* had a good sense of smell and could probably smell its prey before it could see it. It charged prey down at speeds of over 22 miles per hour and ripped it to pieces with its giant teeth. It may also have eaten dead and decaying animals.

Special Features:

- Huge teeth with saw-like edges for biting, gripping and ripping prey
- Powerful legs and small arms with hooked claws
- Holes in the huge skull to make the head lighter

VELOCIRAPTOR

Pack Hunter

These small, but clever and fierce predators, probably hunted in packs, preying on old or weak creatures. They were the inspiration for the raptors in the film *Jurassic Park*.

Fact File

LENGTH: 6 feet

WEIGHT: 55 pounds

NAME MEANS: "Quick plunderer"

PRONUNCIATION: Vell-oss-ee-rap-tore

DINOSAUR FAMILY: Raptors

TIME PERIOD: 70 million years ago

FOSSILS FOUND: China, Mongolia

HABITAT: Dry, semi-desert environment

FAVORITE FOOD: Small animals

FEEDING METHOD: *Velociraptor* probably hunted in packs. In an attack on a prey animal, the huge sickle-shaped claws on each foot were brought forward to slash at the soft parts of the victim.

Special Features:

- Sharp, serrated teeth
- Large, sickle-shaped claw on each foot
- Tail stiffened by bony tendons
- Large brain cavity, which means that it was pretty smart!

Discovery Rating

Fear Factor: 8/10
Defense Factor: 3/10

DiscoveryFact™

The *Jurassic Park* film-makers made the raptors bigger than *Velociraptor* actually was, to make them more scary!

93

INDEX

ANSWERS

Pages 18-19

1. (b) *Camarasaurus*
2. (a) *Elasmosaurus*
3. (b) *Lycorhinus*
4. (a) *Hypsilophodon*
5. (c) *Oviraptor*

Pages 32-33

1. *Euoplocephalus*
2. *Tyrannosaurus rex*
3. *Eudimorphodon*
4. *Diplodocus*
5. *Ichthyosaurus*
6. *Pterodactylus*
7. *Triceratops*
8. *Iguanodon*
9. *Allosaurus*
10. *Oviraptor*

Pages 48-49

1. *Allosaurus*
2. *Baryonyx*
3. *Velociraptor*
4. *Ichthyosaurus*
5. *Oviraptor*

Pages 80-81

1. True 2. False 3. False
4. True 5. False 6. False
7. True 8. False 9. False
10. False